A GIFT FOR:

_____

FROM:

_____

Copyright 2015 Hallmark Licensing, LLC
Published by Hallmark Gift Books,
a division of Hallmark Cards, Inc.,
Kansas City, MO 64141
Visit us on the Web at Hallmark.com.

Editorial Director: Delia Berrigan
Editor: Kim Schworm Acosta
Art Director: Chris Opheim
Designer: Brian Pilachowski
Production Designer: Dan Horton
Writers: Chris Brethwaite, Keely Chace, Allyson Cook, Kevin Dilmore, Russ Ediger, Bill Gray,
Megan Haave, Keion Jackson, Mark Oatman, Tom Shay-Zapien, Dan Taylor, Molly Wigand

ISBN: 978-1-63059-000-0
BOK2247

Made in China
MAY16

FAITHFULLY FUNNY

No, you're **NOT** being **JUDGED**. Really.

Hallmark

GUARDIAN *Angel*

OR

PARTYIN' *Angel?*

BEATRICE
was never sure which one
to listen to.

CLEANLINESS
is next to
MOMliness.

Jacob regretted not being more specific when he prayed for a

PONY.

YES.

CHEESES

LOVE ME.

When Selena and her friends asked themselves

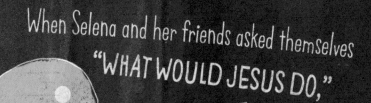

"WHAT WOULD JESUS DO,"

"GO FOR

ICE CREAM"

was ALWAYS the answer.

Because the choir robes were just so

"BLAH."

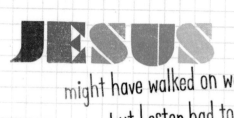 **JESUS** might have walked on water, but Lester had to rely on the **BUS.**

"PLEASE no quilted Bible covers.

PLEASE no quilted Bible covers.

PLEASE..."

Perhaps somebody up there
didn't want them watching

MEN'S BEACH
VOLLEYBALL

after all.

You *can* TALK IN CHURCH. It just takes a a little creativity, that's all.

The church's initiative
to ATTRACT
YOUNGER MEMBERS
was WORKING!

The Hendersons switched to "CONTEMPORARY WORSHIP"
when Bob learned it was code for
"WEAR JEANS TO
CHURCH."

CUTE

WHERE KIDS ARE **PLAYING**, MOMS ARE **PRAYING**.

Every time he caught one,
Mitch would yell,
"OK, NOW WHO
BROUGHT THE
LOAVES?"
Every time.

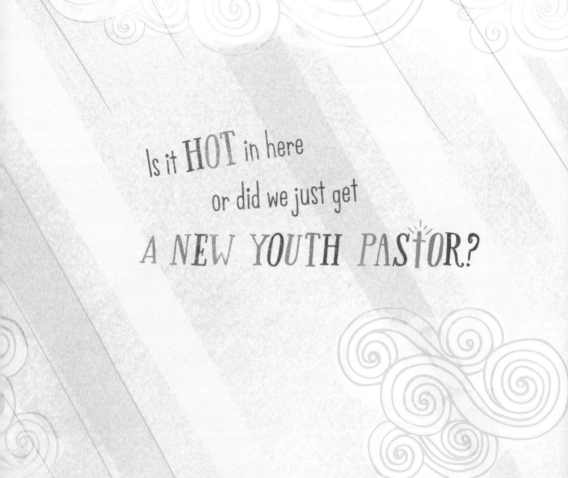

Is it HOT in here
or did we just get
A NEW YOUTH PASTOR?

HE WAS TALL
IN GOD'S EYES,
and that's all that mattered to Donna.

Madge takes great comfort
in knowing
she's just a little closer to GOD
than that gossipy Irene.

"Where in the BIBLE
does it say we have to dress like
DORKS?"

AT

Ralph's Meat Market,

=THEY GAVE UP=

KALE

FOR LENT.

Sarah NEVER prayed for
God to smite her enemies.

NOT OUT LOUD.

The Millers had always

WALKED WITH THE LORD,

though in recent years,

it had become more of

A LEISURELY SHUFFLE.

Marta's not God,
but she does occasionally
OPEN A DOOR
AND CLOSE A WINDOW.

Some moments just

CRY OUT

for prayer.

Once you get hooked on **AMY GRANT,** all other **MUSIC** is just noise.

BLESSED are the PIZZA MAKERS.

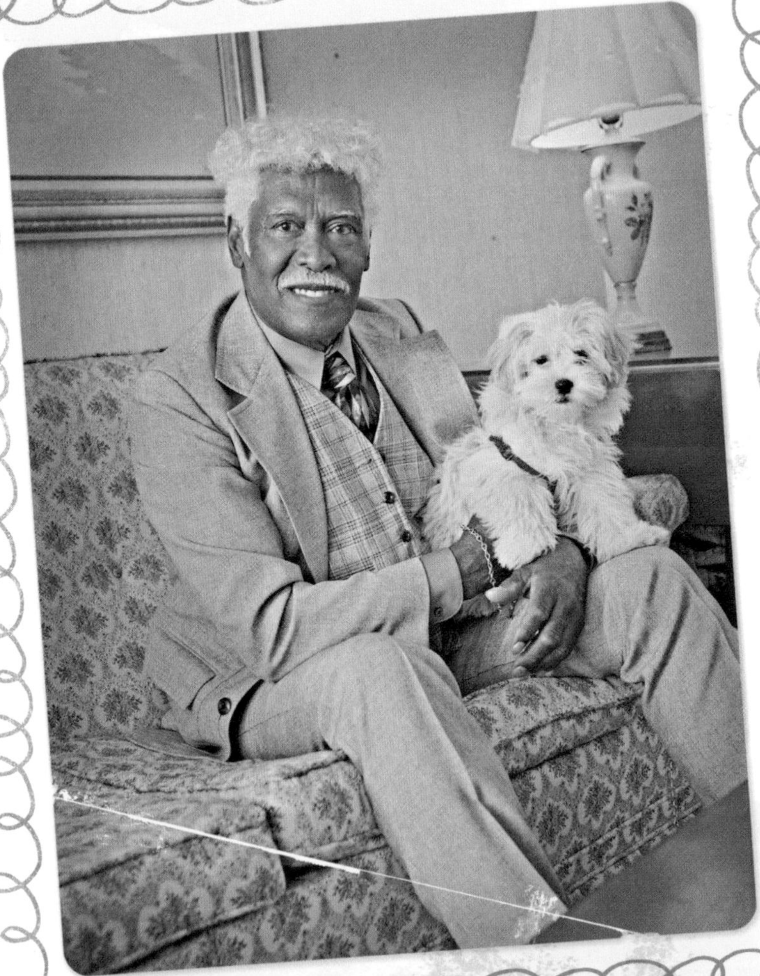

When Uncle Charlie and his dog Teddy
counted their blessings,
GREAT HAIR
 was NO. 1 for both.

EVEN GOD RESTED ON THE SEVENTH DAY.

(The beer was implied.)

The **STEWART FAMILY**
poses with the
less famous
NOT-BURNING BUSH.

No matter
where SUZY sat
in church,
HER PEW
was sure to be
PACKED.

For once,
Sonia felt **CONFIDENT**
that nobody at church
would be **WEARING**
what she was.

Don knows
YOU missed CHURCH
LAST SUNDAY.
Get it together or he's telling
JESUS.

POOR JUDGMENT

is Trevor's

COPILOT.

Knowing life would be hard,
God created something
BEAUTIFUL
to get his people through.
He called it "**BACON.**"

LET FAITH BE YOUR FLOATIES IN THE POOL OF LIFE.

...and the
GEEKS
shall inherit the earth.

Donny liked to think
of his hair as
ICE CREAM SOCIAL
in the FRONT
and PRAYER MEETING
in the BACK.

If you have enjoyed this book
or it has touched your life in some way,
we would love to hear from you.

Please send your comments to:
Hallmark Book Feedback
P.O. Box 419034
Mail Drop 100
Kansas City, MO 64141

Or e-mail us at:
booknotes@hallmark.com